IKHLÂS AND TAQWÂ

SINCERITY AND PIETY

Osman Nûri Topbaş

ERKAM WORLD
INTERNATIONAL ISLAMIC PUBLICATION

IKHLÂS AND TAQWÂ

SINCERITY AND PIETY

Osman Nuri Topbaş

Original Title:	İhlas ve Takva
Author:	Osman Nuri Topbaş
Translator:	Elif Kapıcı
	Zeynep Mahmout
Redactor:	Mustapha Sheikh
Copy Editor:	Adurrahman Candan
Graphics:	Zakir Shadmanov
ISBN:	978-9944-83-137-6
Address:	İkitelli Organize Sanayi Bölgesi
	Mahallesi Atatürk Bulvarı,
	Haseyad 1. Kısım No:60/3-C
	Başakşehir, İstanbul, Turkey
Tel:	(+90-212) 671-0700 pbx
Fax:	(+90-212) 671-0748
E-mail:	info@erkamworld.com
Web site:	www.erkamworld.com
Language:	English

İstanbul - 2023 / 1444 H

CONTENTS

**THE BLESSING OF A PURE HEART:
IKHLÂS AND TAQWÂ-I**

**THE BLESSING OF A PURE HEART:
IKHLÂS AND TAQWÂ-II**

THE BLESSING OF A PURE HEART:
IKHLÂS AND TAQWÂ -III

THE BLESSING OF A PURE HEART:
IKHLÂS AND TAQWÂ -IV

CONTENTS

FOREWORD

Thanks and praises be to Allah Almighty, who has created the creation and made man to be the pinnacle of His divine art, who also revealed to mankind divine knowledge, sincerity (ikhlas) and *taqwâ.*

Greetings and prayers be upon the prophet Muhammad ﷺ, who was the cause of the creation, the light of the candle of love, the sun of guidance and star of gnosis, the highest example of sincerity and *taqwâ.*

Human life is always spent in one way or another. The important thing is how it is spent, in awareness of Allah the almighty and being sincere to him or in ignorance without giving life any meaning.

The most important things that give one's life a meaning are *taqwâ* (piety) and sincerity. *Taqwâ* is to curb one's fleshly desires and to strengthen the spiritual potential through prayers to God and doing good deeds for humanity. Hence *taqwâ* is required in every field of life, in our belief, worship, in our dealings with others, even in our every breath. To have *taqwâ* means to be a friend to Allah almighty, to possess a spiritually healthy heart in this world which can take lessons from the divine manifestations of power in the universe, and to have merit of entering paradise through divine grace.

In other words, to have sincerity and *taqwâ* means to purify our inner world from all kinds of spiritual disease, enabling our hearts to take pleasure from deeds and prayers which are in accordance with the divine will. Such a state of heart is described in the following verse of the holy Quran: "He indeed shall be successful who purifies himself," (Ala, 87:14)

To have sincerity and *taqwâ* means to attain unity with Allah in the heart, which is to assume the divine characteristics of beauty (Jamal) like mercy, forgiveness, slowness in retribution and so on. This means to seek divine satisfaction in all our actions and in all breaths.

Of course in order to attain such high standards one needs to struggle to transform ones heart. Allah almighty explains the difficulty of this spiritual battle by swearing by the seven wonders of creation, at the end of which He tells us that only those who purify their hearts will be saved:

"By the Sun and his (glorious) splendor; By the Moon as she follows him; By the Day as it shows up (the Sun's) glory; By the Night as it conceals it; By the heaven and Him Who made it, By the earth and Him Who extended it, By the soul and Him Who made it perfect, Then He inspired it to understand what is right and wrong for it; He will indeed be successful who purifies it (his inner world), And he will indeed fail who corrupts it. (Shams, 91:1-10)

As these verses show, man has on the one hand his nafs, his egoistic and animal desires, and on the other hand he has the feeling of *taqwâ* that will protect him from his nafs. On the one hand, the nafs which desires to play in the mud, and on the other hand, the soul which desires to fly in the skies.

Rûmî describes this in the following metaphor:

"O traveler of truth! If you want to learn the reality, neither Pharaoh nor Moses is dead, they both live in your body, hidden in your existence. They continue their battle in your heart. Hence you need to search for these two enemies in yourself."

Abu Dharr ❧ narrates the following hadith from the prophet ❧:

One day the Prophet ❧ said: "I know a verse, if people lived according to its meaning; it would be enough (for their salvation).

The companions asked which verse was this and he ❧ answered:

And for those who have *taqwâ* towards Allah, Allah (ever) prepares for him a way out, (Talaq, 65:2) (Ibn Majah, Zuhd, 24)

A man one day came to the Prophet ❧ and asked:

"O messenger of Allah! I am going on a journey, please pray for me."

The Prophet said:

"May Allah give you *taqwâ*!"

The man asked for more prayer from the prophet and He ❧ continued:

"May Allah forgive your sins."

The companion said: My mother and father be sacrificed for you o messenger of Allah please pray for me more:

"May Allah grant you ease wherever you do good" the Prophet said as an answer to this request. (Tirmidhî, Da'awât, 44: 3444).

The basis of the prophet's prayer for the travelling companion was asking *taqwâ* for him first and forgiveness of his sins later and finally the doing of good deeds with ease at all times and in all places. He mentioned *taqwâ* first since only then can one's sins be forgiven and good deeds be done easily.

In order to attain *taqwâ* we need to have a life of contemplation and have awareness. Allah almighty asks in the holy Quran, reminding us of the message of the prophet and of previous prophets:

"Will you not then reflect?" (Hud, 11:30)

"Will you not then understand, will you not use your mind?" (Hud, 51, Muminun, 80)

When man attains the horizon of contemplation, he will continuously ask himself:

"Why did I come into this world? Why do I live? In whose universe am I living? Who is giving me my sustenance?"

Once a man starts asking such questions he will not waste even a second in serving Allah. Although the life is quite short, nevertheless a man has plenty of free time. Warning us about this, the prophet ﷺ said: "There are two blessings which many people lose: (They are) Health and free time for doing good." (Bukhari, riqaq, 1)

If we visualize the terrible states of the judgment day we will not have even a second to lose, in every breath we find a chance to prepare ourselves for the hereafter. Hence it is very important to heed the above and other Quranic messages. Only then can this world be a garden to be harvested in the hereafter. The following verse indicates this fact:

"O ye who believe! Have *taqwâ* towards Allah (Be attached to Allah with sincerity, *taqwâ* and respect, beware of

disobeying him), and let every soul look to what (provision) He has sent forth for the morrow." (Hashr, 59:18)

The second thing in attaining *taqwâ* is to know about the Prophet ﷺ and be acquainted with his life. The companions knew that he was sent as a mercy to all humanity and loved him more than anything else, including their own lives. They followed his example in everything. In addition, they respected anything that belonged to him as a blessing. The following hadith shows the prophet's approval of this as well:

Anas b. Malik ؓ reported that Allah's Apostle ﷺ often visited the house of Umm Sulaym (who was his milk-mother's sister) and slept there while she was away. One day he was sleeping in her house. She came and it was said to her: It is Allah's Apostle ﷺ who is sleeping in your house. She came and found him sweating and his sweat falling on the leather cloth spread on her bed. She opened her scent-bag and began to fill the bottles with it. Allah's Apostle ﷺ was startled and woke up, and said: Umm Sulaym, what are you doing? She said: Allah's Messenger, we seek blessings for our children through it. Thereupon he said: You have done something right.

That was the level of their love for him ﷺ. In the path of guidance the greatest achievement is to share in the spiritual states of the prophet ﷺ. Only with this share will our faith, morality and uprightness be perfected. Therefore we should always ask ourselves the following question:

"Are my states similar to his?"

We should ask this question in every field of life and in every new thing that happens to us. This modest book is a collection of articles written by me in the Turkish monthly magazine Yüzakı, in which we tried to share with the readers as to how *taqwâ* can be practised in different walks of life. May Allah make this work a continuous charity (sadaqa-i jâriya) for those who helped to prepare this work. May Allah create the power of influence over every word said and line written for the sake of truth.

O my Lord! Bless us with shares in the life of the Prophet ﷺ in all our states. Make us attain the highest point of spirituality and identity, giving service to humanity with love. Make us reach the horizons of contemplation, and make us perfect human beings. Make us successful in leading a life of *taqwâ* **and sincerity without even wasting a breath.**

Âmin!

Osman Nûri Topbaş

04.07.2009

Istanbul, Uskudar

The Blessing of a Pure Heart:
Ikhlâs and *Taqwâ-I*

A LIFE OF TRIAL

From among the many millions of living creatures that exist, it was man that Allah chose as the representation of beauty and perfection. He created a being of great honor in the best form (*ahsan taqwîm*), adorning him with many qualities, including intelligence, reasoning and understanding, and blessing him with many abilities. Allah then sent man to earth as a trial for a time. Thus from the time of the first man, Adam, to this very moment, the reason why this perfect creature has been sent to this world is for trial. Every man that has come to this world has endured the same trial and has duly departed; now it is our turn and we are undergoing the very same trial as those who came before us. We should not forget that throughout history the nature of this trial has been the same: how man uses his mind, his intelligence and his understanding, all of which are inclined to both good and evil.

The first duty of man is to pass all of the tests which confront him in this cosmic examination hall that is the world and to become, through them, to become a worthy servant of Allah Almighty.

In this great exam, Allah the Merciful has never left us without guidance - He has sent revelations which contain the profoundest of words in order to guide us and help us to achieve success in this world. He has sent the Qur'ân, the most accurate guide to faith, as a blessing for mankind. He also sent the Prophets, the most outstanding teachers of mankind, as a sign of compassion, to convey the Divine message and explain it to them. He also bestowed upon us, in particular, the additional blessing of being members of the Prophet Muhammad's community (*Ummah*).

Thus achieving success in this world of trials whilst giving praise to our Lord is of the utmost importance. Indeed, the only road to success is to choose to lead a life on the path set out in the final revelation of Allah, the Noble Qur'ân.

A LIFE OF *TAQWÂ*

The essence and meaning of life is found in *taqwâ* and living a life of *taqwâ* essentially means being a true friend of Allah, attaining Paradise and possessing a heart that can understand the deepest depths of Divine blessings. Thus, the truth of *taqwâ* is that one attains a soul that has been purified of all evil and one turns to their Creator with true faith; this is the only way one can reach Allah.

Taqwâ is such an important matter for our happiness in this life and the Hereafter that Allah mentions it in two hundred and fifty eight verses of the Qur'ân providing many directives on how to attain *taqwâ*. In short, Allah wants us to have *taqwâ* at every stage of our lives, in our worship, in our belief and actions, with every breath we take.

What is *Taqwâ?*

The companions of Allah have described *taqwâ* in many different ways. The lexical meaning of *taqwâ* means the avoidance, protection or safeguarding from every kind of evil. That is, *taqwâ* means the protection of Allah.

The term *taqwâ* means being under the protection of Allah by seeking refuge in Him, avoiding what has been forbidden and abiding by what has been commanded; it means fearing the punishment and the torment of the Glorious One and taking refuge in the shadow of His compassion. Therefore, destroying egoistical desires and developing spiritual aptitude is essential. In other words, *taqwâ* is returning to the glory of the orders of the Qur'ân and *Sunnah*, and is the means of eternal bliss in the family, in business and in social life—in short, bliss in every aspect of our lives.

Taqwâ may be described as the execution of the commands of Islam with enthusiasm, reverence and contentment. It means conforming completely with the orders and prohibitions of Allah and avoiding sins at all cost.

Taqwâ is the act of disciplining the soul with the mystery of *"He will prosper who purifies himself"* (Â'lâ, 87: 14) It is when we have done this that our hearts will attain contentment in faith, worship, and deeds which Allah approves of.

Taqwâ is the believer's spiritual union with Allah; it is his manifestation of attributes such as compassion, kindness, forgiveness, mildness and perfection of the heart, as well as the seeking of Allah's acceptance for every deed, every situation and every breath.

Taqwâ is the sincere repentance of the person who is continuously seeking forgiveness with both tongue and heart.

Taqwâ is the heart being full of affection and the fear of Allah's Divine punishment.

Taqwâ is the preservation of the heart from evil thoughts.

Putting knowledge into practice increases a person's wisdom, and the true virtue in protecting the heart is *taqwâ*. This is why the true meaning of faith does not lie in words or rational thought: it is the declaration of the heart's acknowledgement, of applying knowledge in our way of life in such a way as to obtain the approval of Allah. This is only feasible with a soul that is full of the greatest *taqwâ*.

In some way, *taqwâ* is the protection of the heart from anything that distances it from Allah while also being affectionately near anything that will bring it closer to Allah.

Taqwâ means to adhere to the imperative of Allah and His Prophet ﷺ with great love and affection, observing the whole of creation with the compassion and kindness of the Creator, and, being repulsed by anything that is contrary to this, distancing oneself from any situation or action that could damage the soul.

Taqwâ is the manifestation of hatred towards anything that distances the soul from Allah. Therefore, *taqwâ* is destroying egoistical desires and developing the spiritual abilities that Allah has endowed man with.

Taqwâ is a heart that has been assiduously purified; and for those who are successful in such purification, their heart becomes a treasure with the best temperament.

A HEART OF GREAT TEMPERAMENT!

The Prophet Muhammad ﷺ exemplified the nice character traits of the friends of God. Sometimes he would ask his Companions questions that would make the congregation pay greater attention, and in order to elaborate on certain matters. During one of these sessions, the Prophet ﷺ asked the Companions: "Is any one among you capable of being like Abû Damdam?" The Companions said: "Who is Abû Damdam?" The Prophet ﷺ replied: "He was a member of a tribe prior to your time, and he would say, 'I have forgiven all those who have insulted and backbitten me.'" (Abû Dâwud, *Adab* 36: 4887)

This is an example of *taqwâ*: a heart of great temperament!

Hallâj-i Mansûr held his hands up to pray for those who were stoning him, taking refuge in Allah. He pleaded: "O Allah! They are unaware. Before you forgive me, forgive those who stone me!"

Taqwâ is such a great virtue that it brought the Companions close to the Prophet. Anas ﷺ reported that a person asked the Prophet Muhammad: "Who is the family of Muhammad?" and the Prophet replied: "Every pious person is one of my family." Thus we see that a believer who reaches perfection in *taqwâ* is held in such esteem that they are considered to be a member of the Prophet's family.

TAQWÂ CONSISTS OF THREE STAGES:

1 –Avoiding the forbidden.

2 –Aiding by commands. This is a condition to be followed by all believers and is the basic level of *taqwâ*.

3 –Having the feeling of being in the presence of Allah at all times. This is the highest level, the true test of knowledge and *taqwâ*.

In the Qur'ân Allah revealed that He is *"Nearer to [man] than his jugular vein"* (Qâf, 50; 16) and with us as at all times: *"He is with you wheresoever ye may be"* (Hadîd, 57: 4) This unity means that one is adorned with Allah's attributes and is aware of His presence at all times. The soul that is adorned with the garment of *taqwâ* will begin to receive inspiration that direct towards the truth and warn against falsehood and evil; they will realise the real value and meaning of worldly objects. The Qur'ân is a Divine work of art that helps man to resolve every problem he may face. Through the Qur'ân and the *Sunnah* we can gain peace and contentment.

The Qur'ân is the explanation of a person's life. A human's essence is found in the Qur'ân and the Qur'ân is the essence of the whole of humanity; the universe is an endorsement of the Qur'ân.

When a person approaches the pinnacle of *taqwâ*, their perception of the Qur'ân and apprehension of the universe deepens and they become familiar with the wisdom and mystery of the universe. With the singing of the nightingales, the quivering of the rose buds and the steady flow of the streams which bestow the sound of peace, we can gain appreciation of the adornments and blessings of the universe. We begin to

understand the spirit of Yûnus Emre when he spoke with the yellow flower, about the interpretation of his own mysteries.

True *taqwâ* is the sign of having reached Allah. Ibn Atâ'illâh al-Iskandarî stated that a believer who has a sound heart says upon attaining *taqwâ*: "O Allah, what have those who have reached You lost; and what have those who have lost You found?" The rule that all believers should follow is to;

HAVE *TAQWÂ* IN EVERY MATTER

Life passes, with all of its peaks and troughs. Sometimes in hardship and poverty; sometimes in wealth and ease; sometimes with anguish and sorrow; and sometimes our lives are overwhelmed with peace and happiness. During the peaks and troughs of our lives the attitude of a true believer should be that declared by the Prophet: "Be pious in hardship and in ease." The Prophet ﷺ told us that we should not just be believers in certain situations, but rather we should be pious in all matters.

Rûmî says, "Do not be deceived by happiness or affliction, because your soul is just a resting place, and affliction and happiness are only passing guests."

During times of difficulty it is necessary to have patience and seek refuge in Allah without losing one's sense of direction. During times of wealth and abundance one needs to increase thanks for the blessings of Allah without overindulging or boasting to others. We should not destroy our lives by heeding our desires during times of abundance and pleasure. When we are faced with difficulty we should praise and glorify Allah without complaint! Constantly giving praise and gratitude for prosperity and blessings from Allah and submitting to Allah at times of difficulty with patience is a duty of every man. We need to say: "This is what Allah has seen as beneficial for me." This is the test of *taqwâ*.

After winning the great battle of Mecca, the Prophet Muhammad ﷺ reminded the Companions that this was a blessing from Allah and instructed them to give praise and glorify Allah. He reminded them that "true life is the life in Paradise." And again, with the difficulties and trials they faced before the victory at the Battle of the Trench (*Khandaq*), the Prophet Muhammad called on the Companions to have patience saying, "True life is the life in Paradise." The Qur'ân expresses the ways for us to attain a life of *taqwâ* that is expected from us by Allah in many verses. Indeed, the Qur'ân is;

A GUIDE FOR THOSE WITH *TAQWÂ*

Without a doubt, the Qur'ân is a great blessing, a source of spiritual abundance and prosperity for mankind.

"The Most Gracious! It is He who has taught the Qur'ân. He has created man: He has taught him an intelligent speech." (Rahmân, 55: 1-4)

With this revelation Allah states that religion and the Qur'ân are the essence of life for mankind, that they are the reason for creation. Allah the Almighty makes clear that the contents of the glorified Qur'ân, saying: *"This is the Book; in it is guidance without doubt, to those who fear Allah."* (Baqarah, 2: 2) We must scrutinise our actions in accordance with this verse and evaluate our lives by asking ourselves how will we be questioned in the grave and what will our eternal life in the

Hereafter be like? What will our condition be on the Day of Judgment when the universe has been destroyed and where will we be on that day of great power? How should we live in this world in order to survive those moments of horror and the Day of Judgment safely?

What lessons can we gain from the words of 'Umar bin 'Abdulazîz, "Prepare for the Afterlife in accord with how you hope it to be"?

The Qur'ân is our guide in all these questions on the eternal journey; it is the guidance to the questions and their answers, it is the guideline for *taqwâ*. The paths from the heart that lead to the depths of the Qur'ân begin to widen in relation to the level of *taqwâ* reached by a believer. The emotions of a person become refined and delicate and they drift away from egoistical desires, and in so doing become closer to Allah. Allah becomes their "eyes with which they see, their ears with which they hear and their hearts of purity". By doing this, contemplation deepens and becomes conversant with the language of the blooming flowers, the singing birds and the fruit trees. By reflecting this grace, dignity and kindness in their spiritual lives, people are granted souls of goodness.

These are the pious ones who are praised in the Qur'ân. They resemble the flowing rivers that have given life over the years to thousands of living creatures, to humans, trees, roses and flowers of every kind. Their destination is reunion with Allah in the ocean of eternity. Therefore, in essence *taqwâ* is the first step of closeness to Allah. The Qur'ân tells people of *taqwâ* that they should:

SEEK THE MEANS OF APPROACHING HIM

Allah says in the Qur'ân: *"O ye who believe! Do your duty to Allah, seek the means of approach unto Him, and strive (with might and main) in His cause that ye may prosper."* (Mâ'idah, 5: 35)

What are the true ways to come closer to Allah? The purification of the ego, refinement of the soul, obedience, worship, love for the Divine in the heart, the increase of love and fear before His Divine Supremacy.

Allah the Almighty wants us to investigate these means. He has revealed to us that the real goal we should give importance to and concentrate on-our true future-is the Hereafter. This present world is only a tiny drop in the ocean in comparison to eternity. The Qur'ân tells us that on the Day of Judgment we will be asked how we lived our lives. We will answer that we only lived for a day, or half a day. We are required by Allah Almighty to exert ourselves in life to gain even the smallest drop of *taqwâ* that may facilitate for us the attainment of the Ocean of Paradise. But what is the extent of this exertion?

The level of *taqwâ* expected from us is that amount which suffices us to stand before Allah's magnificence in honor and with some worth; that is:

IN REVERENCE TO ALLAH

Allah says in the Qur'ân, *"O ye who believe! Fear Allah as He should be feared"* (Âl 'Imrân, 3: 102) This requires us to "use all our means and efforts to draw close to Allah with our faith, worship and behaviour". Since it is impossible for us to know the appropriate degree of effort needed to stand honourably before the Divine magnificence of Allah, we cannot underestimate the significance of even the smallest deed. Connected to this is the following command: "*And die not except in a state of Islam.*" We can only reach certain places and positions in this world via finite means, and though these positions may be permanent for the duration of our lives, there are no such guarantees in our spiritual lives. The Qur'ân tells us about those who fell into misguidance at the exhalation of their final breath, such people as Bal'am bin Bawra and Qârûn.

Qârûn, a contemporary of Prophet Mûsâ, was the pre-eminent interpreter of the Torah in his time. Allah sent him wealth as a trial. He subsequently became so dependent on that wealth that he arrogantly said to Mûsâ, "Everything is mine. I myself have earned them." So Allah destroyed him and buried him together with his wealth that he had loved and depended on so much. His wealth was of no avail to him within the darkness of the earth.

Bal'am bin Bawra, after having attained various spiritual stations in his lifetime, finally died in a state of misguidane and deviation because he had followed his caprice and ambition and abused his knowledge. As with Qârûn who was destroyed for the abuse of wealth, Bal'am was destroyed for his abuse of knowledge.

Allah commands us to protect ourselves with *taqwâ* when He says *"Serve thy Lord until there come unto thee the Hour that is Certain,"* (Hijr, 15: 99) just as He warns us that protecting the heart with *taqwâ* is a necessity of life.

O Allah! Grant us the ability to abandon everything and stand before you with the true value of *taqwâ*! Prolong our servitude until we take our last breath! And give us the honor of standing before you as members of the community of Muslims!

Âmîn!

The Blessing of a Pure Heart:
Ikhlâs and *Taqwâ*-II

THE SECRET OF SALVATION

Some verses of the Glorious Qur'ân begin with an oath in order to focus the audience's attention on a subject of import. At times, the oath introduces a matter relating to the existence of Allah's servants. There are occasion when the number of oaths increases in harmony with the increased importance of the subject in question. For example, Allah the Exalted begins the ninety-first chapter, al-Shams, with seven oaths. Each introduces one of the wonders of creation-the sun, the moon, the alternation of day and night, the skies, submission and the *nafs*-until, finally, Allah speaks of man's internal struggle and affliction, showing him the only way to salvation: *'By the Soul and the proportion and order given to it. And it's inspiration as to its wrong and to its right; Truly he succeeds that purifies it, and he fails that corrupts it'* (Shams, 91: 7-10).

The Qur'ân makes clear that the human *nafs* has the capacity to be led by its carnal desires and the urge to sin while on the one hand, whilst on the other it possesses the capacity for *taqwâ*. The former tendency is the *nafs'* desire to degenerate in the filth of the world, while the latter is characteristic of a soul that has the desire to spread its wings and take off into the skies.

Rûmî says the following regarding this subject:

"O traveler of truth! If you want to learn the reality, neither Pharaoh nor Moses is dead, they both live in your body, hidden in your existence. They continue their battle in your heart. Hence you need to search for these two enemies in yourself!"

Thus, we can see that *taqwâ* is essential when seeking protection from this enemy of man who confronts him at each and every moment of his life. The Prophet Muhammad's ﷺ asking Allah to bless him with *taqwâ* is an example for believers: "O Allah, Give my soul *taqwâ* and my conscience purity. You are the Master of my soul and the Guardian of my conscience" (Muslim, *Dhikr*, 73). The believer will only be successful in the struggle with his *nafs* if he continues to strive in every aspect of his life; he must live within the boundaries of *taqwâ* in every affair in life, from faith to worship. According to this, one of the main necessities of religion is:

TAQWÂ IN FAITH

If faith is not nourished with *taqwâ* many of the defects inherent in a person's actions will remain; this will result in a weakening of faith and may even render it ultimately useless; a person after this will fall into ignorance and superstition. This is why *taqwâ* is of such great importance.

Taqwâ in faith begins by protecting the *tawhîd* (Divine Oneness) of Allah. The Prophet Muhammad ﷺ said: "Whoever utters *lâ ilâha illallâh* during his last moments in this world will enter Paradise" (Hâkim, *Mustadrak*, I: 503). Yet, how is *tawhîd* protected? The first step in achieving this begins with a true comprehension of the Oneness of Allah. By saying *lâ ilâha*, all idols are removed from the heart in order for the attributes of Beauty to manifest. The attributes of Beauty cannot blossom when the heart is confused, under the influence of sordid ideas, lies in the turmoil of meaningless thoughts or dwells in an alley of blindness. The heart must be purified of negative feelings, negative dispositions and negative habits. Allah the Exalted says: *"Do you see such a one has taken for his god his own passion (or impulse)?"* (Furqân, 25: 43) pointing to the dangers of adhering to negative sentiments and desires of the heart.

The purification of the soul and the perfection of the self are important because the heart is the seat of faith. The roots and essence of faith bloom when the heart is nourished. This is why embedding faith into the soul is essential. Hence believing in Allah is the responsibility of the heart not that of the mind.

The mysteries and the secrets of the cosmos are untangled in accord with the strength of the heart and not the strength of a person's intelligence. Abstruse realities are discovered by the heart. Rûmî says: *"It is impossible to understand the never-ending depth of religion; an enlightened soul can only admire it."* The soul that is open to the discovery of infinite truths is itself a universe full of realities and secrets. Due to the soul's unstable nature and easy change, the greatest difficulty in religion is keeping one's faith after believing in Allah and other divine things. The Prophet ﷺ said, "The heart is like a feather that is being blown about by the wind in a desert" (Ibn Mâjah, *Muqaddimah*, 10; Ahmad, IV: 408, 419). Changes in the heart can cause a diversion in faith. Protecting the heart with *taqwâ* is the only way to preserve faith. Hence, we must be aware;

NOT TO COMPROMISE OR BE INCLINED TOWARDS WHAT IS WRONG

There can be no compromising of faith: one should not incline towards the unbelievers or sinners. One of the characteristics of the heart is that it is influenced by those for whom it feels affection. Thus, Allah Almighty says, *"Incline not to those who do wrong, or the Fire will touch you"* (Hûd, 11: 113), indicating that a believer must protect his soul from the affection of tyrants and sinners. We must never forget that Allah does not want our hearts to be associated with anything other than Himself. The unification of Allah means that we must allow nothing else into the heart; we must not entertain egoistical desires or feel any sympathy for tyrants and sinners. May Allah protect us, particularly from the enemies of belief and against harboring feelings of affection for those who are opposed to Islam for this can only harm the soul. Imâm Ghazâlî says: "Affinity with the ideas of unbelievers over time turns into an affinity of the heart; this affection will become the destruction of a person."

The following warnings of the Prophet Muhammad are of utmost important: "When a sinner is praised Allah becomes angry and the earth trembles" (Bayhaqî, *Shu'ab*, IV: 230).

"Do not call a hypocrite master, because that would make that disbeliever your chief (superior), and you will attract the Wrath of your Creator by so doing" (Abû Dâwud, *Adab*, 83; Ahmad, V: 346).

"Whoever resembles a nation is considered as one of them" (Abû Dâwud, *Libâs*, 4: 4031)

Taqwâ in faith and the protection of the heart is of such importance that the Prophet ordered his companions to participate in fasting on the 10th of Muharram including the day before or the day after in order to differentiate Islamic practice from the practice of the Jews (in Judaism there is a fast only on the 10th of Muharram). Thus, the Prophet Muhammad established a unique basis for the character of Islam and provided us with guidance. To confirm this practice is a requirement of faith, therefore we must take great care in girding our hearts with *taqwâ*. Estrangement of the heart can be compared to mistakenly cutting a main artery with a knife; one would die from the loss of blood. Indiscriminately acquainting the heart with inappropriate people will lead to a loss of purity of the soul and cause it to be absorbed in darkness. The heart is considered the most independent organ in the body as it will keep on beating even after the brain, the "command center", has died. Since this is so, the warning to avoid careless actions is of even greater importance, as Allah the Almighty says in the ninth chapter of the Qur'ân, Tawba, 'O ye who believe! Fear Allah...' (9: 119) In order to protect ourselves from influences that may mislead us we have been given the Divine order:

BE WITH THOSE WHO ARE TRUTHFUL

It is a natural aspect of being human that we are influenced by those with whom we are familiar. Thus, it is necessary to have an awareness of the negative and positive aspects of our environment and of those with whom we spend time.

If one is unaware of the influences they face this can lead to a weakness in *taqwâ* and even guide to destruction.

Taqwâ is protected by guarding the heart against the negative energy of people and by constantly filling the soul with positive energy. There is a current flowing between one heart and another. A simple glance from another person carries a degree of energy sufficient to effect change within us. The energy of the heart, however, is much greater in comparison.

Human beings can be devoted to both the truthful and to those who are oppressors; thus, the protection of truthfulness is achieved by being with those who are truthful and devoted, not with those who are cruel and oppressive.

A dervish once asked Bâyezîd Bistâmî: "Advise me of an action that will bring me closer to Allah." The advice given was: "Love the friends of Allah! Love them so that they will love you. Strive to enter their hearts; Allah looks into the souls of the enlightened ones three hundred and sixty times a day, and if He sees your name in the hearts of just one of them He will forgive you."

The special virtue of the Companions was that they were continuously in the company, or *sohbet,* of the Prophet thus obtaining something of his spirituality and bounty due to Prophethood. The word *sohbet* and *sahabah* (Companions) carry the same meaning; that is sahabah are those who were in the company of the prophet, hence, the physical and spiritual consolidation of the Prophet exalted the Companions. This consolidation has continues on from the time of the Prophet until today.

Sâdî Shirâzî,, explaining the benefits of being with the truthful ones, said: "The dog of the Companions of the Cave (*Ashâb-i kehf*) was granted a great honor because he was among the devoted ones; he has been mentioned in the Qur'ân and in history books."

Rûmî made a similar remark: "*That dog chose to be with the Companions of the Cave. Due to this pleasure he found in their company he will remain in front of the cave until the Day of Judgment. He will be without a dish to eat from but will instead drink the water of compassion and feed on the food of mercy.*" If the soul abandons the truthful ones and instead becomes familiar with sinners and being heedless of Allah then it is doomed. No one of any intelligence, understanding or perception will emerge from these groups or communities. Lût, for example, though he was a prophet, was confronted by the negative energy of his people and thus there was no one in his community able to understand the revelation he received; as a result Lût exclaimed: '*... is there not among you a single right-minded man?*' (Hûd, 11: 78)

In another place, the Qur'ân (Tahrîm, 66: 10) mentions the wives of Nûh and Lût, who chose to be among the sinners rather than with the Prophets, thus being condemned to Hell. Even the wives of the Prophets will not be saved from Divine punishment for their sins. Thus, while at one place in the Qur'ân a mere dog has been given a place of importance, at another two rebellious wives of Prophets have been eternally damned.

Taking this into consideration today where there is little loyalty, in a time when we are approaching the end of the world, *taqwâ* gains even more importance, because holding on to true faith now is

LIKE GRASPING AN EMBER

In a *hadîth*, the Prophet Muhammad said: "Woe to the Arabs, for a great evil is approaching them. It will be like patches of dark night. A man will rise in the morning a believer and become an unbeliever by nightfall. People will sell their religion for a small price. The one who clings to his religion on that day will be like one who is grasping on to an ember." (Ahmad, II: 390; Muslim, *Îmân*, 186; Tirmidhî, *Fitan*, 30: 2196).

In many verses of the Qur'ân good actions are mentioned alongside faith because the lantern of faith is worship and actions; it is for this reason that the second most important degree of *taqwâ* is

TAQWÂ IN WORSHIP, ESPECIALLY IN PRAYER

We will draw closer to *taqwâ* the more that we put care into performing the duties of worship required of us by the fact of our very existence and as part of our servitude to Allah. Only worship that is free of heedlessness and performed with the intention of obtaining the approval of Allah will result in perfection. For example, we know the practical aspects of the prayer; but the real truth of its wisdom is to bring man before Allah. This is a meeting granted to us so that we conquer our spiritual and material needs. Just how close is our prayer to that which has been described and is expected from us by Allah the Merciful? As revealed in the Qur'an, *"Indeed prayer restrains from shameful and evil deeds"* (Ankabût, 29: 45) Are our prayers like this? The following was revealed in the Qur'ân to demand that the heart of a believer be in a state of reunion with Allah when prostrating: *"Prostrate in adoration, and bring thyself the closer (to Allah)!"* ('Alaq, 96: 19) At what level of perfection is our prostration?

The state of our family, our business, and our official duties are all reflections of how we pray. If we pray properly we will have a pious family life, an honest business life and fulfill our official duties in the best way. Allah revealed the following concerning those who do not benefit from the prayer, and whose hearts are full of error: *"Woe to those who pray."* (Mâ'ûn, 107: 4) The Qur'ân focuses our attention on protecting the prayer, its continuity and on submission during its performance. In the same way that physical and spiritual purification is necessary before prayer, submission of the heart is also necessary—the heart must be sensitive and aware that we are standing before Allah. The Prophet Muhammad said, "Allah the Exalted loves every heart that is full of reverence (to Allah), sadness (due to the feeling of not fulfilling the obligations as commanded) and mercy, He loves those who teach people good and call them to obey Allah" (Daylamî, I: 158).

The Prophet ﷺ once saw a man who was fiddling with his beard while praying; he exclaimed, "look and consider, if this man's heart had true submission his limbs would also submit" ('Alî al-Muttaqî, VIII, 197: 22530).

Another example of *taqwâ* in worship is,

TAQWÂ IN FASTING

Fasting is the practice of asceticism, or the minimum use of permitted things, refraining from lawful foods and actions during the day (from dawn to dusk). Perfection and *taqwâ* in fasting requires expanding the conditions of the fast into our

daily lives, living in abstinence from greed, avoiding extravagance and abstaining from what is forbidden or doubtful. The fast shows us how dependant we are on a slice of bread or a glass of water; this is another way that Allah reminds us of just how dependant we are on Him. Those who attain to *taqwâ* in worship also gain the same spiritual feeling from the fast. They are able to contemplate the value of the blessings Allah has given them and feel affection for those who have been deprived in some way. A feeling of mercy and compassion for the hungry increases during the fast and, as a result, this mercy is reflected in charity.

TAQWÂ IN GIVING CHARITY

When giving in charity we should be aware of who this wealth really belongs to. Believers should attain a level where they look at the creation with the eyes of the Creator, that is, with compassion and kindness. This is what we call attaining *taqwâ* in giving charity.

Communists say, "wealth belongs to the community" while the capitalists say "wealth belongs to the individual." Islam declares, "wealth has just been entrusted to human beings; everything is only a temporary provision, the true owner is Allah". Merit comes when the wealth is delivered to its rightful owner. So within these limits, the entrusted one does not have the right to be miserly nor extravagant.

"Do they not know that Allah accepts repentance from His servants and takes the alms, and that Allah is the Oft-returning (to mercy), the Merciful?.." (Tawba, 9: 104) This verse should remain constantly in our minds as the measure of *taqwâ* in aid and charity; this measure is giving without any expecta-

tion or seeking compliments or honor, and with no feeling of pride in the heart. Rather, one should say, "Lillah, O my Lord, this is given only for Your sake". These are the true measures of charity. Allah the Merciful revealed the measure of *taqwâ* and kindness in charity as follows: *"Cancel not your charity by reminders of your generosity or by injury"* (Baqarah, 2: 264). This clearly states the *taqwâ* one should have when giving charity.

Abû l-Layth Samarkandî said: 'The truth about giving in charity is that the person who gives should show gratitude to the one who receives, as with this acceptance the receiver has saved the giver from many kinds of egoistic attachments, as well as strife and calamity; above all, he has gained the pleasure of Allah."

My dear father, Mûsâ Efendi, was very sensitive about the kindness he showed when giving; he wanted to prevent any suffering or shame that the recipients of the charity might feel, and thus he would write on the envelope: 'Dear Mr so-and-so, we thank you for accepting this'. This sincere gratitude from his heart for the receiver was because what was being given was with the hope that Mûsâ Efendi would receive the Divine pleasure and approval of Allah.

May Allah grant us this level of *taqwâ* when giving to charity. Âmîn!

As we have explained previously, *taqwâ* is like a Divine concoction that should be at the base of every religious duty; therefore, the first state we should seek in our worship is *taqwâ*. Hajj is another of the physical religious duties, like charity, which is carried out under the same conditions. The 'wealth' needed by a pilgrim is that which, when he is faced with difficulties whilst in *ihram,* his heart continues in a refined state so that it gains the blessings of Allah.

TAQWÂ DURING THE HAJJ

The Hajj is a demanding duty, both financially and physically; and apart from the financial and physical aspects of the Hajj, the pilgrimage of a person with *taqwâ,* consists of being spiritually present in this holy place and in gaining spiritually. Remembering the days that are experienced while wearing a cloth resembling the death shroud and keeping alive this spiritual feeling is an essential part of the Hajj. We must contemplate the devotion of Ibrâhîm when we stone the Devil. During the Hajj there is to be no unnecessary speech, no sinning and no conflict! We have to avoid situations and actions that distance us from Allah; distancing ourselves from aggressive behavior and arguments and putting this into practice in our daily lives are all the result of attaining *taqwâ* during the Hajj.

While on Hajj it is forbidden to hunt or to pluck a leaf from a living tree. It is even forbidden to tempt a hunter by pointing him in the direction of a potential catch. The purpose is to teach us to extend kindness, gentleness, grace, compassion and sensitivity into our everyday lives. Thus, our religious duties on the whole, including the prayer, fasting, giving charity and performing the Hajj must be performed in a sincere and genuine manner with *taqwâ,* not just on occasion; these qualities must set root in our hearts. If we are not capable of achieving this, this means that the heart has not reached the level of *taqwâ.* A believer must analyse their ego and thus recognise the obstacles that have prevented them from achieving this.

THREE IMPEDIMENTS OF *TAQWÂ*

The first of these impediments is pride; that is, egocentrism. This means that we ascribe our abilities and aptitudes to ourselves though they have actually been granted to us by Allah. We thus act like the Devil, the Pharaoh and Qârûn who also attributed everything to themselves. Hâjî Bayrâm-i Walî said that pride is like a stone tied around the waist; with it you can neither swim nor fly.

The second impediment is miserliness; that is, acting parsimoniously, withholding time or energy for religious duties and daily actions. We should take into consideration the fact that "Paradise is for the generous and Hellfire is for the miserly" (Imâm 'Alî).

The third impediment is foolishness. A person who abandons the Hereafter preferring to accept the blindness of the world, choosing the present life of heedlessness over the eternal universe, can only be a fool.

Concerning those things that can harm *taqwâ*, the Prophet Muhammad said the following words: "There will come such a time when nothing will be dearer than these three things: lawful earnings, true brotherhood and my *Sunnah*" (Haythamî, I: 172). Earning lawful money, enjoying brotherhood based on sincerity and living by the *Sunnah* is only possible with the guidance of truth and good actions. This is why another aspect of *taqwâ* is

TAQWÂ IN CONDUCT

Taqwâ of conduct and sensitivity in every aspect is necessary to ensure bliss and contentment for the individual and the environment. For instance, *taqwâ* in compassion means giving of what you possess to the deprived and less fortunate. In other words, compassion means struggling to help those who have been deprived in the community. Compassion is a believer's conscience of mind in this world and is cause for glad tidings of eternal happiness in the Hereafter. Having mercy is a great blessing from Allah, because it is the result of compassion. Those who pity others are generous, humble and conscious of their duties towards others.

Thus, when in good health, we should contemplate the situation of the disabled, the orphan and the deprived. We must realise that they have been entrusted to us by Allah the Exalted; Allah has sent this people as a trial for us, because a believer is responsible for his brother in faith and humanity.' This is the understanding of Islam.

This is why a believer should hold himself to account at all times and question the degree of compassion that he has. Compassion is the sweetness of faith. *Rahmân*, the Compassionate, and *Rahîm*, the Merciful, are the two most oft-mentioned names of Allah in the Qur'ân; this indicates to us that Allah wishes for the believers to be perfected with the attribute of compassion.

Inspired by a *hadîth*, Rûmî advises the use of compassion by a believer:

"Be compassionate to those less fortunate than you so that those more fortunate than you will show you compassion." The Prophet Muhammad ﷺ said, "I swear by He who holds my soul in His hand, you will not enter Paradise until you believe, and you will not believe until you love each other." The Companions replied, "O Prophet of Allah, we *are* compassionate," in consideration of the compassion they showed towards their children and families. The Prophet replied, "The affection of which I speak is not just for you own kind; this affection includes the whole of creation, yes the whole of creation" (Hâkim, IV, 185: 7310).

It is recorded that while the Prophet was on his way to Mecca together with the Muslim army, he came across a dog at the road-side feeding her puppies. He ordered his army to cross to the other side of the road so as not to disturb the dog and her puppies. On another occasion, when he saw an ants' nest that had been burned out, he cried out: "It is not becoming that anyone except Allah should punish with fire!" (Abû Dâwud, *Jihâd*, 112). If compassion is to be embedded in the soul a person must attain a

STATE OF ALTRUISM (ÎSAR)

The next stage of compassion is altruism; this means thinking of others before thinking of oneself. This is the ultimate level of compassion. It is the state in which Allah loves to see believers. In the Qur'ân, Allah has commended the Ansâr who had shown preference for the Muhâjirûn over themselves. *"Those who before them, had homes (in Madinah) and had adopted the Faith,- show their affection to such as came to them for refuge, and entertain no desire in their hearts for things given to the (latter), but give them preference over themselves, even though poverty was their (own lot). And those saved from the covetousness of their own souls, they are the ones that achieve prosperity."* (Hashr, 59: 9)

This is the great tribute paid to those who have achieved *taqwâ* in compassion and altruism. One of the most significant virtues of the companions of Allah is that they consider others before themselves and their *nafs* is protected against the evil pitfalls of the world by true *taqwâ*.

'Ubaydullâh Ahrâr reported: "A man came and said, 'I am hungry, can you feed me?' I was also hungry, but I had no money or any means to feed myself or him. I took the poor man to a cook and said, 'I have no money but the turban I am wearing is clean. You can use it to dry dishes and in return for this piece of cloth feed this hungry man with some bread.' The cook gave the man a dish of food and even though I was hungry I just sat with him while he ate. Taking off the turban, I gave it to the cook. At first, he refused saying that he did not want it. So I told him: 'I gave you my word, so take it'. After this Allah blessed me with wealth. I had two thousand workers on my farm. Then I took on the responsibility of looking after two men who were unwell. They began to soil themselves due to the severity of their illness. I brought water to clean them; after a while I caught the illness, but I continued to tend them." Look at what a great level of altruism and compassion he showed.

They are the ones who abide by the order *'Spend of your substance!'* (Baqarah, 2: 195). They remain on the path of *taqwâ* with actions of kindness towards all of the creation of Allah. They are the ones of true perfection and benevolence. Thus the essence of *taqwâ* in actions is

TAQWÂ IN IHSÂN (KINDNESS)

The word *ihsân* occurs in various forms over a hundred and ninety times in the Qur'ân. In light of one of its primary meanings, to show kindness, a believer must show kindness in the best possible way in every aspect of his life, whether in his heart, environment, business, or at home. Another of the meanings of *ihsân* is the awareness that every movement is being observed; thus *taqwâ* in kindness and generosity is necessary in every step we take in life.

Finally, the state of a believer should be one of beauty, excellence and perfection at all times. This is achieved through faith and *taqwâ* in submission, and this means that a believer continuously compares his submission to Allah with his submission to humans. Allah describes the condition of a believer's heart in the following verse: 'For, believers are those who, when Allah is mentioned, feel a tremor in their hearts, and when they hear His revelations rehearsed, find their faith strengthened, and put (all) their trust in their Lord.' (Anfâl, 8: 2)

O Allah! Strengthen our faith and deeds with *taqwâ* **and grant us a degree of** *taqwâ* **which is to Your approval. Place us among those whose souls tremble on hearing Your name, those whose faith increases with the reading of every verse of the Qur'ân, and among the ones who worship You alone! Âmîn!**

The Blessing of a Pure Heart:
Ikhlâs and *Taqwâ* -III

TAQWÂ IN CONTENTMENT (RIDÂ)

Situations and incidents occur in four forms: those which are good and those which are evil.

1 –People who are good both inwardly and outwardly:

A person works for a living in an Islamically acceptable job and spends his money for noble causes, continuously giving charity, performing acts of kindness towards fellow humans, animals and the environment with their hands, words and behavior. Such a person is aware of what is unlawful and permitted but also avoids anything that may be doubtful. His heart remains full of *ikhlâs* and *taqwâ*. Such is the manifestation of inward and outward goodness.

2 –People who are evil both inwardly and outwardly:

This is the condition of those who pursue abominations and disgraceful acts in this world. All occurrences of the prohibited, fall within this category. Believing that such a state

of calamity is happiness, they their lives in self-deceit in this world and in the Hereafter they will suffer nothing but grief.

3 – Occurrences which are outwardly good and inwardly evil:

There are some occurrences that seem exceptional when observed externally, yet when examined internally it becomes apparent at the root of their goodness is evil. For instance, wealth which is coupled with a state of indifference to the plight of others because of a dominating *nafs*.

Wealth can seem like a blessing, but miserliness and extravagance in wealth are evils which increase the sins and punishment of a person in both this world and the next. The most significant examples of this are Qârûn and Sâlebe, who were both doomed to perdition. They deceived themselves and persisted in ignoring the commands of Allah in order to gain wealth, thinking it would be beneficial. Rejecting the warnings of the Prophets, they were heedless to the evil of their actions. As a result, both were destroyed in a turbulence of evil that destroyed their lives both in this world and the Hereafter.

The following Qur'ânic verse describes the situation of these people:

"Now, as for man, when his Lord tries him, giving him honor and gifts, then says he, (puffed up), 'My Lord has honored me.' But when he tries him, restricting his subsistence for him, then says he (in despair), 'My Lord has humiliated me!" (Fajr, 89: 15-16)

We should never forget that wealth and poverty are both from Allah; we must comply with whatever Allah sees fit for us and fulfil our duties according to the requirements of whatever we have been granted; this is where true charity begins. If we are heedless to the reality and ignore the Divine will persisting in things that are forbidden, then our situation will be as described in the Qur'ân: *"It is possible that you dislike a thing which is good for you, and that you love a thing which is bad for you. But Allah knows, and you know not."* (Baqarah, 2: 216) The privileged believer is the one who comprehends and lives according to this idea in every aspect of his lives.

The most distinguished quality of the Prophet Muhammad, ﷺ who was blessed with the greatest of human characteristics, was his being the 'most perfect of creation'. The Prophet Sulaymân did not hold on to wealth; he transferred his worldly wealth and goods to the world, and although he lived among so much wealth, he was complimented as being a 'perfect creation' by Allah Almighty. Yûnus was subjected to many trials, deprived of his health, children and wealth for many years; living a life of gratitude and patience, he submitted to his fate, and as a result Allah the Merciful complimented him with being the 'perfect creation' and granted him endless blessings.

4 – Occurrences which are outwardly evil and inwardly good:

A person becomes ill and the deterioration of their health, even though this may seem to be a negative event, becomes a positive event because it is due to this illness that this person begins to understand their own weakness; they seek refuge in Allah, constantly asking for His help through their plight. In this case, the goodness is not manifest.

'Abdullâh ibn Mas'ûd ﷺ said: "I went to see the Prophet, who was suffering from a fever. I said to him, 'O Messenger of Allah, it appears that your fever is intense.' The Prophet replied, 'Yes, I am suffering the pain of two people.' I said to him, 'Perhaps this is so you will gain twice the blessings.' The Prophet responded, 'No calamity befalls a Muslim without Allah expiating some of their sins, even the prick of a thorn'" (Bukhârî, *Mardâ'*, 3, 13, 16).

A true believer should judge the events of this world of trial according to the four truths set out above and continuously take account of the negative qualities of their heart. In every matter they should be aware of their status and the level of repentance, praise and glorification.

Every believer who has *ikhlâs* (sincerity) should make an effort to compensate for the thoughts that occupy his mind, the feelings of his heart, and even the breath that he takes, because pleasing Allah is the greatest fruit of love. The most pleasing to Allah is when a believer abandons the acceptance of their desires and submits to the acceptance of Allah. How, then, are we to recognize good and evil when they are not ostensible in order that we can reach this kind of contentment? This question has but a single response:

GOODNESS IS WITH ALLAH ALONE

In his work *Âmâk-i Hayal*, a book of sufi wisdom, written by Ahmet Hilmi Efendi of Filibe, there are two important characters; one is Aynali Baba, who is a Gnostic illuminating people with his wise words accompanied by the play of Ney (flute). Another character is Raji who is a seeker of truth. They often come together and Aynali Baba plays Ney, they discuss things about the universe and the purpose of life. At one of such meetings, whilst Râjî was listening to Aynali Baba playing the *ney* he fell in to a deep sleep. He found himself in a gathering of many people from Prophets to philosophers, important personages to ordinary people. A man stood to speak on behalf of mankind. In tears, he asked the great thinkers of the world the way to true happiness: "Tell me, please have compassion; I hate my life but I cannot abandon it. Please tell me what happiness is."

Some of the people there answered. Confucius said, "Happiness is cooking rice to just the right consistency." Plato said, "It is to think always about nobility." Aristotle said, "It is logic! That is what happiness is." Zoroastra said, "It is not being left alone in the dark." Brahma said, "Happiness? Happiness is the antithesis of what everyone thinks." Buddha stood up in a rage: "O humanity! Happiness is one of the beautiful names of non-existence, Nirvana. O humanity, stick to Nirvana!" The people who heard this were confused and said, "You have not helped yourselves; you have lived your lives deprived of happiness and there is not even a trace of happiness in what you preach!"

Just then a friend of Allah stood up and said, "For the intelligent, happiness is observing Divine beauty, whereas for the ignorant, it is greed and lust!" In fact, he had disclosed happiness as taught by the Prophets. Finally, the head of the gathering, the Pride of Creation ﷺ, stood up and said, "O Humanity! Happiness is accepting life for what it is, accepting burden and hardship, and making every effort to improve; in other words, happiness is obtaining a heart of purity." Having found the answer they were looking for, the people stood up and chanted, "O Honored one of the universes! The greatest Prophet! *You* are the only one who can understand and find the cure for humanity!"

Rûmî, the great guide, was a prolific reader of people's lives: he was fully aware that goodness came only from Allah. He said, "Until you accept or are content with that which Allah has sent, no matter where you run in the hope of salvation, know that you will face calamity; without a doubt, disaster will come and find you. There is not one corner of the universe that is free from the pitfalls of evil. There is no contentment or salvation in this world other than living within one's spiritual peace; thus, seek Allah in your soul and take refuge in Him. There is no place in this dungeon of the worlf, where protection money is not demanded and men are not beaten on every corner.

"I swear by Allah that if you seek refuge in a mouse hole you will be caught by the cat; the only way out is by being a sincere believer and reaching Allah. He will console and protect you against the snakes and scorpions. In the end He will become your friend."

Once, a jinn came in the form of a snake to 'Abdulqâdir Gaylânî, the great spiritual guide. It departed as his friend. This is an example of the blessing which are brought by Divine love and contentment.

Therefore, the duty of a believer who has asked for eternal goodness in life is to accept all that they face with *taqwâ*, except disbelief and straying from the path. If life is experienced in this way, death and the afterlife will be of benefit and man will prosper on the Day of Judgment.

Another condition of reaching this level of temperament is repentance and forgiveness. The character of the soul that is required by Allah the Merciful is

TAQWÂ IN SEEKING FORGIVENESS AND REPENTING

A condition of repentance is that one's remorse is sincere; pursuing *taqwâ* in repentance ensures that one will return to Allah in a state of purity with a permanent repulsion for sin. The essence of *taqwâ* in repentance is fulfilling this promise with righteous actions. When a believer removes the curtains of blindness from their soul they are aware of the burden of sin on their conscience and awaken to a sense of prosperity in the heart. The soul turns to Allah with tears of regret; this is the true repentance from errors and a sign of genuine remorse. This is the path back to Allah.

Thus, repentance is the removal, through a feeling of remorse, of the obstacles that exist between the believer and Creator; the secret of repentance is having a forgiving heart. One who forgives becomes worthy of forgiveness; another dimension of *taqwâ* in seeking forgiveness is that when a person asks to be pardoned they consider their own ability to forgive others, and by continuously forgiving others they earn the right to be forgiven.

The following advice from Hadrat Alî to a person who was appointed as governor is very significant: "Do not look at human beings like a wolf with its sights on a herd! Have love, affection and kindness towards them from the heart! Without exception, they are either your brethren in faith or fellow human beings; they can make mistakes. Help those who are in need and if you ask for forgiveness from Allah you must also forgive; forgive and be tolerant towards them! Never be heedless, or challenge the orders of Allah! Never renege on your forgiveness! And do not take pleasure in punishments you have to give!"

Abû Dardâ, ﷺ one of the Companions of the Prophet, was a judge in Damascus when he heard some people swearing and shouting at a sinner. Abû Dardâ asked them, "What would you do if you saw that a man had fallen into a well?" They answered, "We would throw him a rope and try to save him." Abû Dardâ ﷺ then said, "Then why are you not trying to help this man who has fallen into the well of sin?" They were so surprised that they asked, "Do you not feel angry towards this sinner?" Abû Dardâ ﷺ gave an answer of great wisdom, "I despise his sins, not his person."

There is great wisdom in Abû Dardâ's ﷺ desire to embed this principle into the souls of believers. This wisdom has a divine glimmer of the commands and pleasure of Allah; it reflects the character of the Prophet into the souls of the community. The only way to attain eternal pleasure in this mortal world is to be like the Prophet and spread the fragrance of forgiveness and love from the soul; when we are faced by undesirable incidents we should turn our hearts into an abode of wisdom that is full of the Divine blessings that smell the fragrance of Paradise, accompanied by forgiveness, friendship, kindness, tolerance and humility.

The beautiful quality of *taqwâ* encourages man to think about others. The human character that is most loved by Allah is that which struggles to help and save others. In particular,

ENCOURAGING WHAT IS GOOD
AND FORBIDDING WHAT IS EVIL

Encouraging good and forbidding evil are the most important characteristics of a believer. The duty of a pious person is to express this with their actions as well as their speech and to advise good and prevent evil in a gentle manner. If the invitation towards Islam and the fear of Allah is abandoned the community will become vulnerable to disasters. Zaineb bint Jahsh reported that she asked the Prophet of Allah, "O Messenger of Allah, while the believers are among us will we be destroyed?" The Prophet ﷺ replied, "If sins and abomination proliferate, then yes" (Bukhârî, *Anbiyâ'*, 7). Therefore, the only way to protect ourselves against Divine punishment is to encourage others to do good and to forbid them from evil; this is the task of every believer with *taqwâ*. While performing this duty or any related duty, one must be guided by the Qur'ân and *Sunnah*, and consult a person of knowledge at every stage. Hadrat Alî gave the following advice to a governor: "Do not accept into the committee for consultations those who threaten you with poverty or try to prevent you from doing good actions; do not accept cowards who try to increase your ambition or those who have been blinded due to their greed!"

"Turn to Allah and his Messenger for solutions to the problems you cannot solve! Refer to Allah and His book and refer to the Prophet Muhammad and his *Sunnah*."

If we desire to be from "the best nation" we must live a virtuous life and advise others to live in goodness, abstaining from bad and evil and prohibiting others from doing the same. We have to be aware of our duties on the path of Allah; without this sense of duty and affection a person cannot be successful in advising others of what is good and what is evil. What is essential is

TAQWÂ WHEN WORKING
IN THE SERVICE OF ISLAM (KHIDMA)

The basis of all principles of Islam is turning towards Allah with true affection and sincerity, *ikhlâs*. Without doubt, the only way to achieve this is through servanthood. Those who work in the service of Islam spread great energy around them that everything finds life through them; by enlightening their environment, they increase their own illumination. Sincere service is the result of a sound heart. Success in servitude requires knowledge, wisdom, efficiency, equanimity and a responsible character and personality. The heart of a dutiful person should be like fertile soil; those who derive benefit from it leave behind ashes; by purifying the ashes the soul is able to cultivate various plants that will nourish all the passing creatures. Therefore, those who do not have sufficient knowledge or experience, who give no importance to the progress of spirituality or morality, those dutiful ones who have no true understanding cannot offer service of any use; we cannot expect any good to come from service that has been performed in a harsh manner by abrupt and offensive people who are not blessed with a heart of good temperament.

Therefore, service that has been deprived of the soulful bounties is like a bucket of water that is poured into an arid desert or a seed thrown into a scorched field; it will fall to field mice, doomed to failure; the seeds of duty that are planted by the heart will become blossoming trees in the future.

The greatest duty towards human beings, within these measures, is to assist them in attaining the eternal future. The only way to achieve this is by being guided to the path of a true believer by the principles and guidance of the Qur'ân. The following prayer of the Prophet ﷺ should be in the hearts and prayers of those who continuously perform their duties as human beings: "O Allah! I seek refuge in you from helplessness, idleness, cowardice and every kind of weakness." This prayer of the Prophet ﷺ emphasizes the need for sensitivity and thoughtfulness, as well as action.

According to this, those who help others must show kindness and every action should be performed with the greatest caution.

Being acquainted with those we help is a duty that is as great as the mission itself to ensure that it is given to those who are most worthy. Sometimes helping one person of good character can be equal to helping thousands of people; if you supply the means to an intelligent person it will never be wasted. Another important point to consider when helping others is to act with feelings of gratitude. Sheikh Sâdî said, "Glorify Allah for making you successful in your good deeds, because Allah has granted His benefaction and blessings upon you. The servants should not expect the Sultan be grateful for their service to him, on the contrary they should be grateful that He has employed them."

We should be aware that the essence of this benevolence is found in our duty to Allah and His Prophet ﷺ because a pious man knows that he has reached *taqwâ* with the blessings that have been granted by Allah and His Messenger. In the same way, it is this person's responsibility to enforce this duty on others. One of the most intense feelings in the heart should be

TAQWÂ IN LOYALTY

The basic meaning of loyalty is to neither forget nor neglect a friend; all friendships should continue with the bond of loyalty. When the feeling of loyalty fades then friendship also fades, and when loyalty dies out friendship comes to an end. It is possible to say that Allah's Prophet lived his whole life as the greatest example of loyalty. He was loyal to his wet nurse who brought him up, he was loyal to the Abyssinians who protected the Muslims when they migrated there, he was loyal to Khadîjah who believed in him while others called him a liar and he was loyal to all his Companions. He was especially loyal to Allah the Merciful; this was a very different type of loyalty and was apparent with every breath the Prophet took.

'Â'isha ﷺ reports that an old lady came to the Prophet one day when he was in her company. He asked the old lady to introduce herself. The woman said, "I am Jassâmah (lit. huge in size) of Muzan." Because her name implied a negative attribute, the Prophet ﷺ changed it saying, "No, from now on you are Hassânah (lit. beauty, elegance) of Muzan." Then he asked her how she had been keeping since he had last seen her. She replied, "All praise to Allah, my family and I are fine, may my mother and father be sacrificed for you!" When the woman left, 'Â'isha asked the Prophet what was the cause of his immense respect for that woman. The Prophet of Allah answered: "She would come to us often when Khadîjah was alive, and loyalty is a part of faith" (Hâkim, I, 62: 40). Those who were

refined through the Prophet's great manners became symbols of loyalty themselves.

Unfortunately, morality with such virtue is a thing of the past; it is not something that is found in the heart in its true form anymore. It is a mere word ornamenting the dictionaries now. Without a doubt, this is due to a decline in the fear of Allah. "For everyone who breaks his promise, there will be a flag (to mark him out) on the Day of Judgment, and it will be announced that this flag is the symbol of the promise made by this person" (Bukhârî, *Jizya*, 22; *Adab*, 99; *Hiyal*, 99; Muslim, *Jihâd*, 11-17).

It must be emphasized that our first and primary duty of loyalty is to Allah and then to His Noble Prophet, ﷺ who is the reason for our creation, our eternal happiness and our path to faith. Loyalty thereafter should go to the great ones of faith who have taught and guided us to the straight path, then to our mothers and fathers, whom we must serve while they are alive. Being polite and honoring our parents is the greatest debt of loyalty shouldered by a son or daughter.

Loyalty to our elders, to the dead and to the living, loyalty to the nation and to all of society is also the quality of a positive character. Therefore, every believer should protect his *taqwâ*, never surrendering to the chaos of the present time, and never abandoning efforts to repay the debt of loyalty; otherwise, affection loses its true value and so does friendship and servitude. It is the duty of a human being to guard their *taqwâ* in loyalty. We must realize, however, that the condition of *taqwâ* in loyalty is:

TAQWÂ IN LOVE AND AFFECTION

We cannot achieve anything without love and affection in our hearts; even the smallest of deeds requires the support of affection. In the same way, the secret of our creation, the secret of our actions, is affection. This affection must be developed within the boundaries of *taqwâ* because it is necessary to support affection with true values. The first of those we truly love must be Allah the Merciful and His Prophet. ﷺ Allah granted believers the emotion of love so that they could be affectionate between themselves as Muslim brothers. Loathing negative things is essential for the protection of affection . Good and evil become apparent according to affection. The degree of a person's affection is like the one they love; people admire that for which they feel affection and follow them as an example; indeed a person is influenced by those they love. The Companions of the Prophet were distinguished in every matter and place because of their affection for and the blessings of the Prophet Muhammad. ﷺ Companions who were nearby also acquired something of the high morality of the Prophet; the Muslims in the Hunayn valley gained courage from him, and the Companions acquired their submission to acceptance of Allah from him. In short, the status and prosperity in belief, worship, family life, loyalty and kindness of the Companions was a reflection of the Prophet. ﷺ The Companions actually became what they were through this affection.

At the time of the Prophet's death, the Companions were bent in grief. Those adoring souls that could not bear to live without seeing him for a day were now never to see him in this world again. It is very interesting that at this time, 'Abdullâh bin Zayd, who could not bear the thought that he would never see the Prophet in this world again, held his hands up in prayer and pleaded from his pure heart: "O Allah! Take my sight! I do not wish to see anything in this world if I cannot see the dear Prophet whom I love so much!" He immediately lost his sight. Directing our affection towards Allah requires loving the light of Muhammad and his blessed person, loving the Companions of Allah, and then expanding out further and loving every creature of Allah. The greatest and most meaningful manifestation of affection for the Prophet is his sunnah. In accordance with the maxim "the lover adores everything that belongs to the beloved", following the prophet, the beloved of Allah is essential. To the same degree that we can reach the 'essence of Muhammad' using our intelligence, we can also reach it with affection. We must never forget that the love and affection we feel for anyone else in the universe other than Allah is 'figurative love', while the deep love and affection we feel for the Lord of the Universe is the 'Real Love'. In this sense, *taqwâ* is to avoid anything that will distance us from Allah Almighty and the Prophet; this can be achieved by loving those who Allah and the Prophet love and disliking those whom Allah and His Messenger disapprove.

O Allah! Make us love those whom You love and dislike those of whom You disapprove! Never deprive us of servanthood, affection or loyalty to You or to Your Noble Prophet! Grant us a love for the truth within the bounds of *taqwâ*! And place us in both worlds with the Noble Prophet!

Âmîn!

The Blessing of a Pure Heart:
Ikhlâs and Taqwâ -IV

TAQWÂ IN SINCERITY (*IKHLÂS*):

Ikhlâs is a necessary prerequisite for good deeds and actions to be accepted by Allah. *Ikhlâs* is that these actions are performed solely for Divine acceptance with all egotistical intent eliminated. *Ikhlâs* means protecting the heart from every kind of worldly gain in order to be closer to Allah. *Ikhlâs* is such a great blessing for actions that without it salvation is not possible. Actions without *ikhlâs* are empty, deprived of all goodness. In essence, *ikhlâs* is a secret of Allah and obtaining this secret through *taqwâ* should be the aim of every believer, because this is the basis of piety.

If a believer is sincere in their *taqwâ*, that is, if their *taqwâ* has *ikhlâs*, then this means that they are pious in every matter. But, what is *taqwâ* in *ikhlâs*? Among the explanations, one is that the spiritual and physical nature of a person corresponds with one another, and that person is sincere and acts in an honest manner, making great efforts to prevent selfishness, hypocrisy, insincerity, and pride, all of which can destroy his *ikhlâs*.

Hadrat Alî, ﷺ speaking to the same governor mentioned above, gave great words of advice: "Do not praise yourself! Do not respect anyone who praises you to your face! Do not remind others of what you have done for them! Do not exaggerate those things at which you are successful! Do not break promises! Reproaches destroy goodness, exaggeration kills the truth, and not keeping a promise will instigate the abhorrence of Allah and the community."

We should remember that the Prophet forbade boasting, because he was aware that everything was a blessing from Allah. At Khandaq (the battle of Ditch), the moment when the Companions had begun to give up hope, during their greatest times of hardship, when they were wondered if the help of Allah was on its way, the Prophet Muhammad ﷺ told them, "True life is life in Paradise." Then again, this time in Mecca, at their time of victory, the Prophet Muhammad said, "True life is life in Paradise," showing that he completely trusted in and submitted to Allah.

The Prophet Muhammad knew that victory and accomplishments, wealth, life and children-in short, everything-comes from Allah. *Taqwâ* is foundational because in both this world and the next, the essence of peace is

TAQWÂ IN WEALTH, LIFE AND CHILDREN

These are the most important things to man, the things that most depend on us and those which greatly affect our souls. It is important to use and steer these in the way of Allah, spending life and wealth generously, raising children with faith to be beneficial for Islam, country and community, leaving behind a spiritual heritage for future generations. Allah states the measure of our affection in one of the verses of the Qur'ân: "*By no means shall ye attain righteousness unless ye give (freely) of that which ye love.*"

So the best of wealth is that which reaches the Hereafter before its owner does and the best form of life is that which is put to use in pursuit of Allah's pleasure and acceptance. Those who know how to make use of their wealth and life are as shining lights; their goodness and good deeds illuminate even the darkest places and the light of their prosperity and generosity is spread to the needy, to the deprived and to the weariest of souls. A child's obligation is to make every effort to attain the assent of their parents, while the parents are obliged to gain the approval of Allah.

The truth of the matter is that even if it seems that our wealth and blessings in this life come from our mothers, our fathers or ourselves, they are in fact an entrustment from Allah. Thus, our duty is to have

TAQWÂ IN LOOKING AFTER TRUSTS

All that which is between the Heavens and the earth has been entrusted to humans by Allah the Merciful; that is, the whole of creation has been entrusted to us. Everything in the universe was created for mankind and so all are a trust. Thus, we must show all of them affection, for is this not why the Prophet ﷺ said, 'If you must kill a snake which is attacking you then kill it with one strike so that it will not suffer"?

The most important of trusts are the Qur'ân and the *Sunnah*, so let us remember the declaration made by the Prophet Muhammad ﷺ during his last sermon: "O believers, I am leaving behind two precious things, the Qur'ân and my *Sunnah*. If you adhere to them both you will never go astray." This means that the most important thing entrusted to us is our duty of representing Islam by adhering to the Qur'ân and the *Sunnah*, in our faith, deeds, states and behavior. In every situation we confront, Allah the Almighty and His Prophet expect us to display the kind, dignified and mature heart of a Muslim so that others will comment, "What a good person this Muslim is!"

The Qur'ân was not given as a trust to Muslims so that it could be left on a shelf or recited now and again at funerals and other occasions. Allah the Merciful has ordered us to read (*iqra'*) the Qur'ân. To have secrets disclosed and the wisdom of the Qur'ân, we have been ordered to study the *Sunnah* of the Prophet. Also in the Qur'ân is the statement: "*Fear Allah and Allah will teach you.*" (Baqarah, 2: 282)

If we live within the bounds of *taqwâ*, with every passing day more secrets of the Quran will be unveiled. It is our responsibility to understand this and the trusts bestowed upon us because those who await guidance at every place in the world have been entrusted to us; the poor are a trust, the lonely are a trust, the desolate and the orphans are a trust. The riches of the world have been entrusted to us, our children have been entrusted to us; in short, everything has been entrusted to us. It is revealed in the Qur'ân: "*He has subjected to you, as from Him, all that is in the heavens and on earth: behold, in that are Signs indeed for those who reflect.*" (Jâthiya, 45: 13)

It is a form of compassion to return these trusts to their rightful owner. Therefore, those who attain high statuses-whether spiritually, financially, intellectually or in the service of society-must realise that this position is a temporary assignment of entrustment. They should not become attached to their positions for they will not remain there eternally. On the other hand, in the same way that wasting material things has been prohibited in Islam, the waste of spiritual provisions like faith, worship, knowledge, time and intelligence is also proscribed; in fact, these are seen as the greatest danger. The whole point is to protect our trusts with *taqwâ*, and this requires a sense of responsibility. Thus, another aspect of *taqwâ* is

TAQWÂ IN RESPONSIBILITY

All deeds, actions and duties flourish with an awareness of responsibility. Without a doubt, Allah has blessed human beings with capabilities and every individual is only responsible for the ability that they have been given. We are all aware that we have to give 1/40th in charity, but it is never possible to know the measure of the ability that we have been granted by Allah. This is why Allah does not want us to waste our strength unnecessarily. He tells us: *"Strive together (as in a race) towards all that is good"* (Baqarah, 2: 148) and *"Fear Allah as He should be feared and die not expect in a state of Islam."* (Âl 'Imrân, 3: 102)

A believer must be aware of how he should live and in what conditions he should die. He should know how to educate himself so as to obtain the benevolence of faith. Every breath we take follows the previous one and is a preparation for our lives in the Hereafter; therefore, these breaths must be used to improve our actions. To ensure a life of bliss that is adorned with good deeds, it is necessary to live in prosperity and peace on the path of Allah in this world; living a life that is unacceptable to Allah is like a mirage in the desert. There are appointed times for religious duties, whereas faith and servitude are a duty at all times throughout our lives. Our life in this world is just a specified period given to prepare for the Hereafter, where we can gain Divine acceptance.

The path to Divine union is a narrow crossing which is full of trials and hazards; the responsibilities are so great that they turned the hair of the Prophet white:

THE WAY OUT IS *TAQWÂ*

According to a report from Abû Dharr, one day the Prophet said, "I know a verse of the Qur'ân that, if the people were to adhere to it, it would be sufficient for the whole of mankind." The Companions asked, "O Messenger of Allah, which verse is it?" The Prophet of Allah recited, "*...And for those who fear Allah, He (ever) prepares a way out*" (Talâq, 65: 2; *hadîth* in İbn Mâjah, *Zuhd*, 24).

The 'way out' might be explained as the way from hardship to contentment, from the earth to heaven, from futility to worth or to superiority; hence the basis of worthiness in Islam is

SUPERIORITY OF *TAQWÂ*

The Prophet of Allah addressed Abû Dharr, explaining that the only standard of value and acceptance in the sight of Allah is *taqwâ*. "A white man has no superiority over a black man except in *taqwâ*" (Ahmad, V, 158).

On another occasion, the Prophet said, "I have the most *taqwâ* amongst you."(Bukhârî, *Îmân*, 13; Muslim, *Siyâm*, 74) He acted within the bounds of *taqwâ* in every aspect of his life. Thus, it is essential that we be pious believers who conform to the

Sunnah of the Prophet Muhammad. ﷺ Compliance with this and similar conditions is

THE INDICATION OF *TAQWÂ*

Prophet Isâ described *taqwâ* beautifully. One day, someone came up to him and asked, "O master of goodness, how can a human have *taqwâ* before God?" Jesus answered, "This is easy. Love God with your heart and do good deeds according to your ability. Show compassion and kindness to all the sons of Adam as if you were sorry for yourself!" Then, later he said, "Do unto others as you would have others do unto you! You will then be truly pious in the eyes of Allah!" (Ahmad, *Zuhd*, p.59).

The essence of our actions and worship should generate the observation among the angels that;

THIS IS *TAQWÂ*!

One day, 'Umar ﷺ asked Ubayy bin Ka'b ﷺ what *taqwâ* was. Ubayy said, "O, 'Umar, have you ever walked down a path of thorns?" 'Umar answered, "Yes I have." Ubayy asked, "And what did you do?" 'Umar said, "I pulled my clothes tightly and walked carefully to avoid the thorns." Ubayy bin Ka'b then said, "This is what *taqwâ* is" (Ibn Kathîr, *Tafsîr al-Qur'ân al-karîm*, I: 42).

The sun that will rise above us if we live with this degree of *taqwâ* will be,

THE SUN OF *TAQWÂ*

'Abdulqâdir Gaylânî gave the following advice regarding *taqwâ*: "O son, *taqwâ* is essential; make every effort to obtain *taqwâ* so that your soul will be freed of its inner hostility and evil ways and thus turn to goodness. O son! When you gather worldly assets, do not be like the one who gathers wood at night, unaware of what he is gathering. Take great care to understand if these worldly belongings are lawful or prohibited, legitimate or illegal, and abide by *tawhîd* and *taqwâ* at every moment." The essence of this advice was the prayer of the Prophet for *taqwâ*

"MAY ALLAH GRANT YOU *TAQWÂ*"

A man came to the Prophet and said, "O Prophet of Allah, I am going on a journey. Will you pray for me?" The Prophet replied, "May Allah grant you *taqwâ*." The man then said, "O Prophet of Allah, pray a little more for me!" The Prophet responded, "May Allah forgive your sins." The Companion said, "O Messenger of Allah, pray a little more, may my mother and father be your ransom," The most noble of creation then said, "May Allah grant you ease wherever you do good" (Tirmidhî, *Da'awât*, 44: 3444).

The intent of these prayers was to convey the importance of *taqwâ*; first he asked Allah to give *taqwâ* to those who asked for a prayer, then he asked for forgiveness for their sins and ease in their good deeds. The reason he prayed in this way was that these things can only happen if a person has *taqwâ* of the soul; without *taqwâ* sins will not be forgiven nor can righteous deeds be carried out. This is why Allah wants us to be pious and puts us through trials of *taqwâ* in all of our actions and deeds. The trial of our devotion, affection and respect of the Prophet is named as the

TRIAL OF *TAQWÂ*

The following is a verse of the Qur'ân: *"Those that lower their voice in the presence of Allah's Messenger,- their hearts has Allah tested for taqwâ. For them is forgiveness and a great reward. Those who shout out to thee from without the inner apartments, most of them lack understanding."* (Hujurât, 49: 3-4)

This means that the courtesy we show towards the Prophet Muhammad, ﷺ the fact that we follow his actions and way of life, and that we are aware of him, are all trials of *taqwâ* for our souls; it is a chance to appreciate our love for him while being closer to Allah at the same time. So *taqwâ* in our every day actions, from faith to good deeds, must be the garment of our souls.

THE GARMENT OF *TAQWÂ*

"O children of Adam! We have bestowed raiment upon you to cover your shame, as well as to be an adornment to you, but the raiment of righteousness- that is the best" (A'râf, 7: 26). The raiment, or garment, of *taqwâ* is the only true garment that adorned the souls of the Prophets and friends of Allah. The following is a well-known report: One day Imâm Abû Hanî-fah was busy cleaning a tiny spot of dirt from his clothing. A few of his companions, not seeing the need for this, said, "O Imâm, according to your interpretation of Islamic law, this stain does not prevent you from praying, so why are you going to so much trouble?" The Imâm answered, "That may be Islamic law but this is *taqwâ*."

Living life devoted to Allah is living according to the following verse of the Qur'an in every aspect of life: *"Therefore stand firm (in the straight path) as thou art commanded"* (Hûd, 11: 112).

Allah the Almighty not only expects us to perform actions that are good, He also takes into consideration and observes our degree of *taqwâ*. Therefore, it is possible to say that religiousness is a lifetime of *taqwâ* and the compassion and protection of Allah is for believers who work to obtain the acceptance of Allah with true piety. All the Divine goodness of this world and the Hereafter belong to the pious ones. Therefore, purifying the heart of sin and evil through *taqwâ* is true bliss and the way of salvation for mankind. Our only spiritual provision is

THE PROVISION OF *TAQWÂ*

The more a person's love and knowledge of Allah increases, the more his *taqwâ* increases; and this is what is expected of us, because it is the *taqwâ* of the heart that reaches Allah from all righteous actions.. It is revealed in the Qur'ân that, *"It is not meat or the blood [of the sacrificial animals] that reaches Allah: it is your taqwâ that reaches Him"* (Hajj, 22: 37)

Rûmî warned us of this reality, saying: "Do not attempt to sacrifice the shadow of the goat!" *Taqwâ* of this kind is not that which is recognized by the intellect but; it is that which is felt and practiced from the heart. With regard to this, Allah revealed: *"Is one who worships devoutly during the hours of the night prostrating himself or standing (in adoration), who takes heed of the Hereafter, and who places his hope in the Mercy of his Lord (like one who does not)? Say: 'Are those equal, those who know and those who do not know?' It is those who are endued with understanding that receive admonition."* (Zumar, 39: 9)

Alongside this knowledge, we must:

1. Prostrate before Allah at night.

2. Stand in worship.

3. Protect ourselves from the punishment in the Hereafter, (not neglecting mortality).

4. Ask for the compassion of Allah.

Only the knowledgeable ones who have these qualities should be respected. The virtue of this reality is related in the following *hadîth*: "Those who increase their knowledge but not their *taqwâ* distance themselves from Allah." This is why Allah does not expect us to prepare for the Hereafter with material provisions or physical objects; the one provision that He requires of us is the provision of *taqwâ*. Much like purchasing a new car and neglecting to put petrol in it, only the possession of dry knowledge will be of use on the journey to Eternity. As you can see, *taqwâ* is of prime importance for the eternal journey. In the Qur'ân we read, *"Take a provision (with you) for the journey, but the best of provisions is right conduct. So fear Me, O ye that are wise"* (Baqarah, 2: 197).

How contented are those who take the journey to eternity with the provision of *taqwâ*!

O Allah! Grant us the provision of *taqwâ*—*the taqwâ* **of the Prophets—with our every breath; endow us with it as a garment for our souls eternally! End our lives in bliss and include us in Your Divine acceptance and goodness! Give us health and make our** *taqwâ* **a provision on the true path to eternity!**

Âmîn!